"Two Giants Comp ',
Linux vs.

Presenter: Ronin RX"

COPYRIGHT

DEDICATION

Dear Readers, I hope you have enjoyed this journey through the world of operating systems, exploring the differences and similarities between Linux and Windows. It has been an honor to guide you through this fascinating territory of computing.

The choice between Linux and Windows is a pivotal decision in the digital world. I hope that through the pages of this book, you have gained a deeper and valuable perspective on which of these two giants best suits your needs and preferences.

Remember that in the ever-evolving technological world, knowledge is power. As you continue to explore and use these operating systems, I encourage you to stay informed about the latest trends and developments. Never stop learning and growing in your understanding of technology.

If this book has sparked your curiosity or a desire to delve even deeper, consider revisiting my future publications. Technology continues to advance, and I look forward to sharing more knowledge and insights with you in the future.

Thank you for investing your time and energy in "Two Giants Compete for Supremacy, Linux vs. Windows." I hope you have found this journey as enriching as I have. Until the next page, where we will continue exploring the exciting world of technology together. With gratitude and best wishes.

RONIN RX, FROM GAMING RX"

INDEX

INDEX

Introduction

Presentation of the importance of choosing the Linux or Windows operating system.

Part 1

The choice of the operating system, whether it's Linux or Windows, is a critical decision that impacts individuals and organizations in a variety of ways. Both operating systems have their own advantages and disadvantages, and the choice between them largely depends on the specific needs and preferences of each user. Below, I present the importance of choosing between Linux and Windows:

Linux:

1. Open-source software: Linux is an open-source operating system, which means that its source code is accessible and modifiable by anyone. This promotes transparency and allow users to customize it to their needs.

2. Security: Linux is known for its robust security. Since it is less vulnerable to malware and viruses compared to Windows, it is a popular choice for servers and security-critical environments.

3. Variety of distributions: Linux offers a wide variety of distributions (distros) that are optimized for different use cases. This provides great flexibility in choosing the version that best suits your needs.

4. Cost: Most Linux distributions are open-source and free, which can result in significant cost savings compared to Windows licensing.

5. Performance: Linux tends to be more resource-efficient, making it ideal for older or hardware-limited computers.

Introduction

Introduction to the importance of choosing between the Linux and Windows operating systems.

Part 2

Windows:

Software Compatibility: Windows is widely used in the business world and offers a wide range of commercial software and applications, making it ideal for businesses and users who rely on specific Windows applications.

User-Friendliness: Windows is known for its intuitive and user-friendly interface, making it suitable for non-technical users. Most people are familiar with Windows due to its widespread adoption.

Technical Support and Updates: Microsoft provides strong technical support and regular security updates for Windows, ensuring that the system is protected against current threats.

Gaming: Windows is the dominant platform for PC gaming, with a vast library of games and greater hardware support for gaming.

Interoperability: Windows offers better integration with other Microsoft products, such as Microsoft Office and Exchange, which can be essential for businesses relying on these applications.

In summary, the choice between Linux and Windows depends on the specific needs of each user or organization. Linux is ideal for those who value customization, security, and lower costs, while Windows is the preferred choice when specific software compatibility, user-friendliness, and reliable technical support are needed. In many cases, it is also possible to use both operating systems in a dual-boot configuration to harness the best of both worlds.

The History of Linux and Windows

Dear readers, this is a fascinating narrative that spans decades of development and competition in the world of operating systems. These two operating systems are iconic in the world of computing and have evolved independently, offering users diverse and unique options. In the following four pages, we will explore the history and evolution of Linux and Windows, highlighting the most significant milestones in the development of both systems.

The Birthplace of Operating Systems Linux: The Birth of a Giant The history of Linux begins in 1991 when a young Finnish programmer named Linus Torvalds developed an operating system kernel inspired by Unix. This kernel, named "Linux," was based on the Free Software Foundation (FSF) GNU project and quickly gained followers in the open-source software community. Collaboration from developers worldwide led to a robust, versatile, and open-source operating system that we know today as Linux.

Windows: Microsoft's Takeoff On the other hand, Windows is the product of Microsoft, one of the most influential technology companies in history. Their first operating system, MS-DOS, was released in 1981. However, it was in 1985 when Microsoft released Windows 1.0, marking the beginning of their journey into the world of graphical user interfaces. Since then, Windows has be an integral part of personal and business computing.

Battles for Market Domination Linux: The Open Source Revolution Linux gained popularity in the 1990s thanks to its open-source General Public License (GPL), which allowed anyone to modify and distribute the system. Companies and governments began adopting Linux due to its flexibility and security, leading to the creation of numerous distributions like Ubuntu and Red Hat. Today, Linux is the predominant operating system on servers and is used in a variety of devices, from mobile phones to smart appliances.

Windows: Desktop Dominance Microsoft Windows dominated the desktop operating system mar in the 1990s and early 2000s, with iconic versions like Windows 95, Windows XP, and Windows Although Windows has faced challenges in terms of security and stability, it remains the primary choice for most PC users worldwide. Competition from macOS and Linux has driven Microsoft to improve its operating systems over the years.

New Directions and Challenges

Linux: Diversification and Business Success As Linux grew in popularity, many companies adopted this operating system for their servers and data centers due to its stability and low cost. Additionally, the rise of Android, an operating system based on the Linux kernel, made it the most widely used operating system on mobile devices. Linux has also expanded into areas such as the cloud and supercomputing, serving as the foundation for systems like IBM Watson and the Tianhe-2 Supercomputer.

Windows: The Challenge of the Modern Era In the modern era of computing, Microsoft faces new challenges. The proliferation of mobile devices and the growing competition from systems like macOS and Linux have led the company to focus on platform convergence. Windows 10 introduced a unified approach to mobile and desktop devices, and Windows 11 continues this trend with a more modern design and productivity-oriented features.

An Evolving Future Linux: Continuous Innovation and Diversity The world of Linux is diverse and constantly evolving. The development community continues to innovate in areas such as artificial intelligence, automation, and security. Moreover, Linux adoption in the enterprise and cloud environments continues to grow. Linux distributions remain an attractive choice for servers and embedded systems, and the success of Android has further solidified Linux's position in the mobile device market.

Windows: Adoption of New Business Models Microsoft continues to adapt to a rapidly changing technology landscape. With the transition to subscription models like Microsoft 365 and cloud services like Azure, the company is shifting toward a cloud and mobility-focused approach. Windows 10 and Windows 11 are designed to be more secure and flexible, and Microsoft remains committed to innovation in areas such as artificial intelligence and augmented reality.

In summary, Linux and Windows are two operating systems that have made a significant impact on the field of computing and technology. Linux, with its emphasis on open-source code and global collaboration, has proven to be a dominant force in servers and embedded systems. Windows, on the other hand, has maintained its supremacy in the world of desktop operating systems and has evolved to meet the challenges of the modern era.

Both operating systems continue to develop and adapt to a constantly changing technological world, and it is exciting to imagine how they will continue to evolve in the years to come. The choice between Linux and Windows ultimately depends on individual needs and preferences, and each offers a unique set of advantages and challenges for users and businesses.

Underlying Architecture
"Details about the fundamental architecture of Linux and Windows"

Introduction to Linux

Linux is an open-source operating system based on the Linux kernel, developed by Linus Torvalds in 1991. Over the decades, it has evolved and become one of the most widely used operating systems in the world, largely due to its flexible and high-performance architecture.

Linux Kernel

At the core of Linux is the kernel, which is responsible for managing hardware resources and providing an interface for applications and services. The Linux kernel is monolithic, which means it contains a significant amount of kernel space code that interacts directly with hardware. This allows for high performance but also requires careful management of kernel drivers and modules.

Layered Model

The architecture of Linux follows a layered model. On top of the kernel, there is the user space, where applications and services reside. Essential services such as the file system, process management, and memory management are provided in user space through system libraries and utilities. The interface between user space and the kernel is achieved through system calls.

Linux Distributions

Linux is distributed in various distributions, or "distros," which include the Linux kernel and a set of utilities and applications designed to meet specific needs. Some of the popular distributions include Ubuntu, Fedora, CentOS, and Debian. Each of these distributions adapts the underlying architecture of Linux to meet the requirements of its target audience.

Underlying Architecture of Windows

Introduction to Windows

Windows is an operating system developed by Microsoft that has become an integral part of most personal and business computers. Throughout its versions, it has evolved considerably, but its underlying architecture has remained largely constant.

Windows Kernel

The Windows kernel is the fundamental component that manages hardware and provides essential services. Unlike Linux, Windows uses a hybrid kernel that combines features of both a monolithic and microkernel. This allows for greater modularity and reliability by isolating critical components.

Architecture Model

Windows follows a layered architecture model similar to that of Linux. The Windows kernel provides services such as process management, file system, memory management, and security. Above the kernel is the user space, where applications and services run. Windows provides a rich API for applications to interact with the operating system.

Versions and Editions

Windows is offered in a variety of versions and editions, including Windows 10, Windows 11, Windows Server, and more. Each edition is tailored to specific needs, from desktop systems to enterprise environments.

Comparison of Linux and Windows Key Differences

• **License:** Linux is open-source and distributed under various licenses, allowing for extensive customization and community development.

Windows is a commercial, proprietary product of Microsoft.

• **Kernel:** Linux uses a monolithic kernel, while Windows uses a hybrid kernel, which affects modularity and flexibility.

• **Distributions** vs. 10, 11, and older versions Versions: Linux is distributed in multiple distros, each tailored for a specific purpose, while Windows comes in different versions and editions with specific features and focuses.

Similarities

• Both operating systems offer a graphical user interface and a command line.

• They provide file and directory management, allowing users to organize and access data.

• They are compatible with a wide range of applications and services, including web browsers, office software, and development tools.

In summary, both Linux and Windows have robust underlying architectures that enable users and developers to make the most of their features. The choice between the two often depends on the specific needs of the user and personal preferences. Both operating systems have had a significant influence on modern computing and will continue to be integral in the future.

Process and Resource Management

Explanation of how each system manages system processes and resources.

ocess and resource management in Linux and Windows operating systems is essential for the
ficient operation of computers. Each operating system has its specific approach and methods to
ndle these aspects. Below, I will provide a detailed explanation of how Linux and Windows
anage system processes and resources.

troduction Process and resource management are fundamental aspects of any operating system, as
ey allow multiple applications to run simultaneously on a computer. In this document, we will
plore how Linux and Windows address process and resource management.

ocess Management in Linux and Windows Linux: Linux uses a Unix-based approach to process
anagement. Each process in Linux is identified by a unique number called a PID (Process
entifier). The Linux kernel creates and controls processes.

ocesses can be divided into parent and child processes, allowing the creation of process
erarchies.

dditionally, Linux allows for the creation of lightweight processes called "threads" that share
sources with other threads of the same process.

nux also provides commands and tools like ps, top, and htop to monitor and manage processes in
al-time.

ocesses can be backgrounded or foregrounded, enabling users to interact with multiple
plications simultaneously.

indows: Windows manages processes by creating a process table that contains information about
ch running process.

ch process is identified by a unique identification number called a PID. Windows uses a window-
sed approach, meaning that programs have a graphical user interface (GUI) that allows users to
teract with them.

e Windows Task Manager is a widely used tool for monitoring and managing processes.

rthermore, Windows allows the creation of threads, which are smaller units within a process and
n share resources with other threads of the same process.

Resource Management in Linux and Windows

Linux: In Linux, resource management is based on the principle that "everything is a file." This means that everything in the system, including hardware devices, is represented as files in the virtual file system /proc and /sys. Resources such as CPU and memory are allocated to processes through task schedulers and memory managers.

Linux offers a range of commands and utilities for resource management, such as "nice" and "renice" for adjusting the priority of a process and "ulimit" for setting limits on the resources a process can use.

Windows: In Windows, resource management is accomplished through the Task Manager and the Task Scheduler. Task Manager allows users to view and manage real-time CPU, memory, and other resource usage by processes and applications.

Windows utilizes the Task Scheduler to automate tasks in the system. Users can schedule tasks to run at specific times or in response to certain events.

Page 4: Conclusions and Comparison

In summary, both Linux and Windows are widely used operating systems that effectively manage processes and resources, though with different approaches:

- Linux employs a Unix-based approach with a virtual file system that treats everything as files and provides a wide array of command-line commands and tools for process and resource management.
- Windows relies on a graphical user interface (GUI) for managing processes and resources and offers tools such as Task Manager and Task Scheduler to monitor and automate tasks.

The choice between Linux and Windows depends on specific needs and user preferences. Both operating systems are highly functional and can meet a variety of requirements.

Ultimately, process and resource management are essential to ensure efficient system performance and a smooth user experience on any platform. Linux and Windows offer distinct approaches to achieving these goals, providing users with flexible options based on their needs and preferences.

Security A detailed analysis of the differences in security approaches between Linux and Windows.

Comparing security approaches between Linux and Windows is a fundamental topic in the field of cybersecurity and system administration. Both operating systems have their own features, strengths, and weaknesses when it comes to security. In this detailed analysis, we will explore the key differences between Linux and Windows in terms of security in four fundamental areas:

• Architecture

• User and permission management

• Security updates

• Known vulnerabilities

Architecture:

Linux and Windows have fundamentally different architectures, which significantly influence their security approaches. Linux uses a "multi-user and multitasking" type of architecture from its inception. This means that multiple users can share the system simultaneously, and each has their isolated space. Security in Linux is heavily based on privilege separation and file permission structure. The Linux kernel is monolithic, which allows for greater flexibility but also carries a higher risk if an attacker gains superuser access. On the other hand, Windows has a more user-interface-oriented architecture. Originally designed as a single-user operating system, it has evolved to support multiple users but still tends to be more susceptible to attacks due to its historical design. User and permission management in Windows can be more complex compared to Linux, potentially leading to misconfigurations that expose vulnerabilities.

User and Permission Management:

User and permission management is a critical aspect of security in both operating systems. In Linux, user management is based on the "least privilege" principle. Regular users have limited access and can only make changes to their files and configurations. To perform administrative tasks, it is necessary to access the superuser (root) account. This limits the attack surface, as an attacker needs to bypass the security of the superuser account to make significant changes to the system.

In Windows, user management tends to be more complex, as there are various account types, such as standard user accounts, administrators, and system accounts. Security is based on the User Account Control (UAC) model, which requests confirmation for high-risk actions. However, users often have the option to bypass these prompts, which can be dangerous.

15

Security Updates

Both Linux and Windows offer regular security updates, but they differ in how they are handled.

Linux has package management systems like APT (Advanced Package Tool) and YUM (Yellowdog Updater, Modified), which allow administrators to quickly update all system software with a single command. This makes it easier to apply security patches and keep the system up to date. Additionally, Linux distributions often have active development communities that respond promptly to vulnerabilities.

In Windows, security updates are managed through Windows Update. While Microsoft also provides regular updates, the experience may vary depending on the Windows version and user update policies. Sometimes, updates are postponed or not applied in a timely manner, leaving systems unprotected.

Known Vulnerabilities:
Linux and Windows have experienced known vulnerabilities over the years, although they differ in the quantity and impact of these vulnerabilities.

Linux tends to be less vulnerable to malware attacks, in part due to its permission structure and open-source approach. However, it is not exempt from vulnerabilities. Some popular distributions like Ubuntu and Red Hat have dedicated security teams that respond to threats and release patches quickly.

Windows, due to its widespread adoption in the business and consumer world, is a constant target for attackers. Vulnerabilities in Windows often have a significant impact. Microsoft also responds to these threats with patches and updates, but the diversity of versions and configurations can make some systems more vulnerable than others.

In summary, both Linux and Windows have robust security approaches, but they differ in terms of architecture, user management, security updates, and known vulnerabilities.

The choice between them will depend on the specific security needs of an organization or user, as well as the ability to properly manage and maintain the system.

It is important to remember that no operating system is completely immune to threats, and effective security requires a combination of good management practices, proper configuration, and constant monitoring.

Performance, Discussion on How Performance Differences Affect Daily Use
Part 1

The comparison between Linux and Windows in terms of performance is a broad topic and can vary depending on various circumstances, including hardware configuration, user needs, and specific versions of the operating systems. Here, I will present a general discussion on how performance differences affect daily use in both operating systems:

Kernel and File System:
• Linux: The Linux kernel is known for its efficiency and resource management capabilities.
• It uses file systems like ext4 that are efficient and robust.
• This results in fast and reliable performance.
• Windows: Windows has also improved its performance over the years, but its kernel and file system can be less efficient compared to Linux. NTFS, the default file system, tends to slow down over time.

Hardware Requirements:
• Linux: Generally, Linux tends to be lighter in terms of hardware requirements compared to Windows. It can perform well on older systems or systems with limited resources.
• Windows: Windows usually requires more powerful hardware to run optimally, especially with the latest versions. This can affect users with older hardware.

Updates and Maintenance:
• Linux: Updates in Linux can be managed more flexibly. Users can choose when and how to apply updates, allowing better control over system performance.
• Windows: Windows tends to have more intrusive updates, which can temporarily affect system performance. However, these updates are essential for security.

Rendimiento, Discusión sobre cómo afectan las diferencias de rendimiento al uso diario
Parte 2

Compatibilidad de Software:
• Linux: La mayoría del software de Linux es de código abierto y optimizado para funcionar bien en el sistema. Sin embargo, algunos programas populares de Windows no están disponibles o pueden requerir emulación.

• Windows: Windows tiene una amplia base de usuarios y, por lo tanto, una amplia gama de software compatible. Sin embargo, algunos programas pueden ser más exigentes en términos de recursos.

5. Seguridad y Estabilidad:
• Linux: Es conocido por su estabilidad y seguridad. Los sistemas Linux son menos propensos a virus y malware, lo que reduce la carga del sistema en términos de seguridad.

• Windows: Windows es más vulnerable a virus y malware, lo que puede ralentizar el sistema debido a la necesidad de software de seguridad adicional.

6. Personalización:
• Linux: Linux es altamente personalizable, lo que permite a los usuarios optimizar su sistema para el rendimiento. Pueden elegir entornos de escritorio ligeros y ajustar configuraciones para mejorar el rendimiento.

• Windows: Windows ofrece cierta personalización, pero es menos flexible que Linux en este aspecto.

En resumen, la elección entre Linux y Windows en términos de rendimiento dependerá de las necesidades del usuario y el hardware disponible. Linux suele ser una excelente opción para sistemas con recursos limitados y para aquellos que valoran la personalización y la estabilidad. Windows, por otro lado, es más adecuado para usuarios que necesitan un amplio acceso a software de terceros y no les importa invertir en hardware más potente.

Flexibility and Customization in Linux
Part 1

Exploring why Linux is appreciated for its flexibility and how Linux users can customize it. Linux is widely known and appreciated for its flexibility and customization. This distinctive feature of Linux is derived from its open-source nature and modular structure. Let's explore why Linux is appreciated for its flexibility and how users can customize it:

1. Open Source: Linux is an open-source operating system, which means its source code is available for anyone to modify and redistribute. This allows users to tailor the operating system to their specific needs. They can change and improve any aspect of the system, from the kernel to the user interface.

2. Variety of Distributions: Linux is not a single operating system but a family of systems based on the Linux kernel. There are numerous Linux distributions (distros) such as Ubuntu, Debian, Fedora, CentOS, and many more. Each of these distros is designed to meet specific needs, whether for servers, workstations, desktop environments, or embedded systems.

3. Customizable Desktop Environments: In Linux, desktop environments like GNOME, KDE, XFCE, and others are highly customizable. Users can change themes, icons, wallpapers, and window layouts to adapt their working environment to their personal preferences.

4. Customized Packages and Software: Linux package management systems like APT, YUM, and Pacman allow users to install, update, and uninstall software efficiently. Additionally, users can compile software from its source code, giving them greater control over configuration options and library compatibility.

Flexibility and Customization in Linux
Part 2

5. Customizable Shell: Linux offers a variety of command-line shells, such as Bash, Zsh, an Fish. Users can customize their shell by creating scripts, aliases, and personalized configurations to automate tasks and enhance efficiency.

6. Total System Control: Linux users have complete control over their system. They can fine tune kernel settings, manage services, configure firewalls, and control file and directory permissions meticulously.

7. Development and Programming: Linux is the preferred choice of many developers and programmers due to its open-source software development tools. Users can customize the development environment to meet their needs, which is crucial for custom software development.

8. Security and Privacy: Users can customize security and privacy policies in Linux. They ca choose how updates are managed, which services run, and how their data is encrypted. In summary, the flexibility and customization in Linux result from its open-source nature, th wide variety of distributions, and users' ability to modify nearly any aspect of the system. This allows people to tailor Linux to their specific needs, whether in terms of performanc appearance, or security. Linux has become a powerful and highly adaptable platform that caters to a wide range of users, from enthusiasts to developers and businesses.

Description of Windows familiarity and its compatibility with popular applications. Windows is one of the most popular and widely used operating systems in the world. Its familiarity and compatibility with a wide range of applications are two key reasons for its success.

Here is a description of Windows familiarity and its compatibility with popular applications:

Familiarity in Windows

Familiar User Interface:
Windows has maintained a consistent user interface across various versions, especially with the introduction of the Start Menu in Windows 95. Users have come to know and expect certain elements, such as the desktop, the taskbar, and the File Explorer.

Shortcuts and Hotkeys:
Windows uses common shortcuts and hotkeys that users have learned over time. For example, using Ctrl+C to copy, Ctrl+V to paste, and Ctrl+Z to undo are standards in many Windows applications.

Compatibility with Drivers and Hardware:
Windows has broad compatibility with a variety of devices and hardware. Hardware manufacturers often release specific drivers for Windows, making it easy to install and operate devices on Windows systems.

Large User Base:
The large number of Windows users makes it easy to find online resources, tutorials, and solutions to common problems. The Windows user community is sizable and active, making it easy to get help online.

Compatibility with popular applications

1. **Microsoft Office:** Microsoft Office is one of the most widely used productivity suites in the world, and Windows offers excellent compatibility with these applications, including Word, Excel, and PowerPoint.

2. **Web browsers:** Windows is compatible with a wide range of popular web browsers such as Google Chrome, Mozilla Firefox, Microsoft Edge, and others, allowing users to choose the one that best suits their needs.

3. **Design and editing software:** Popular applications like Adobe Photoshop, Adobe Illustrator, and CorelDRAW are available for Windows and are commonly used in fields such as graphic design and image editing.

4. **Games:** Windows is a leading gaming platform, with broad compatibility for a variety of games, from traditional PC titles to Microsoft Store games and Steam titles.

5. **Business and productivity software:** Windows is widely compatible with business and productivity applications, such as enterprise management software, accounting software, and collaboration tools.

In summary, the familiarity of Windows and its extensive compatibility with popular applications are key factors that have contributed to its ongoing success as an operating system. Users find that Windows is an environment in which they feel comfortable and that allows them to use a wide range of essential applications for their daily needs.

Ejemplos Prácticos
Parte 1

Muestra de casos de uso y ejemplos prácticos para ilustrar las diferencias. De linux y Windos

Linux y Windows son dos sistemas operativos con diferencias significativas en su funcionamiento y en la forma en que los usuarios interactúan con ellos. A continuación, te presento algunos ejemplos prácticos que ilustran estas diferencias:
1. Instalación de Software:

Linux:

En Linux, puedes usar un administrador de paquetes (como APT en Ubuntu o YUM en Fedora) para instalar software. Por ejemplo, para instalar el navegador web Firefox en Ubuntu, ejecutas el comando sudo apt-get install firefox.
Windows:

En Windows, generalmente descargas e instalas software desde sitios web o utilizas herramientas como el Windows Store. Para instalar Firefox, descargas el instalador desde el sitio web de Mozilla y sigues un proceso de instalación más tradicional.

2. Actualizaciones del Sistema:

Linux: En Linux, las actualizaciones del sistema y del software se gestionan a través del administrador de paquetes. Puedes actualizar todo el sistema con un solo comando, como sudo apt-get update && sudo apt-get upgrade en Ubuntu.
Windows:

En Windows, las actualizaciones del sistema operativo se gestionan a través de Windows Update, mientras que las actualizaciones de aplicaciones se gestionan individualmente por las aplicaciones o la tienda de aplicaciones de Windows.

3. Sistema de Archivos:

•Linux: Linux utiliza una estructura de directorios jerárquica, donde / es el directorio raíz. Los archivos y directorios están organizados en una sola estructura.
•Windows: Windows utiliza unidades de disco (C:, D:, etc.) y una estructura de directorios con una jerarquía diferente. Por ejemplo, C:\Users\NombreDeUsuario/ Documentos es una ubicación común para los documentos de usuario en Windows.

Practical Examples

Part 2

4. Terminal Access:
• **Linux:** Linux offers a command-line terminal, such as Bash, which provides a high level of control over the system. Users can execute commands to perform advanced tasks. Windows: Windows also has a command-line interface, namely the Command Prompt or PowerShell, but most users interact with the graphical user interface.

5. Licensing:
•**Linux:** Most Linux distributions are open-source and free. You can use, modify, and distribute Linux freely.

•**Windows:** Windows is a proprietary operating system from Microsoft that requires licenses. To use Windows, you need to purchase a license or use a trial version for a limited time.

6. User Management:
•**Linux:** In Linux, users and groups are managed through commands in the terminal. You can easily create, delete, and modify users and groups.

•**Windows:** In Windows, user management is done through the Control Panel and the user account settings in the graphical interface. These examples illustrate some of the key differences between Linux and Windows in terms of software installation, system administration, directory structure, and other areas. Each operating system has its own advantages and disadvantages, and the choice between them depends on individual needs and preferences.

User Communities

Discussion about user communities and online support for both platforms.

User communities and online support are essential aspects in the world of Linux and Windows.

Both operating systems have active communities that provide help and share knowledge through forums, discussion groups, social networks, and other means. Here are some key considerations for both platforms.

Linux User Communities:

Discussion Forums:
•Linux has numerous online forums where users can ask questions, get technical assistance, and share experiences. Examples include the Ubuntu forum, LinuxQuestions.org, and Stack Exchange.

Distribution-Specific:
•Each Linux distribution (such as Ubuntu, Fedora, or Debian) has its own user community and support forums, allowing users to get specific help for issues related to that distribution.

IRC Channel:
Many Linux projects have real-time chat channels on Internet Relay Chat (IRC) where users can ask questions and get immediate assistance.

Wikis and Documentation:
•Most Linux distributions have online wikis and documentation that explain how to perform specific tasks, solve problems, and configure software.

Events and Conferences:
Linux conferences and events, such as LinuxCon, provide an opportunity to learn from experts and connect with other Linux enthusiasts.

Communities of Windows Users

Microsoft Support Forums:
•Microsoft provides online support forums where users can ask questions about Windows, Offic
and other Microsoft products.

Specialized Websites:
•Websites like Bleeping Computer, TenForums, and Tom's Hardware have active communities
where users can get help with Windows and related hardware issues.

Reddit:
•Platforms like the r/Windows subreddit provide a space for discussions, tips, and problem-
solving related to Windows.

Microsoft Documentation:
•The Microsoft website offers detailed documentation, guides, and articles on how to use and
troubleshoot their products.

Events and Conferences:
•Microsoft and other Windows-related events, such as Microsoft Ignite, allow IT professionals
and advanced users to learn about the latest developments and connect with the community.

•In summary, both Linux and Windows have active online user communities that provide suppo
and resources for problem-solving, learning, and knowledge sharing. The choice between these
platforms often depends on specific needs and personal preferences.

Implementation Decisions

Tips for choosing an operating system based on user needs (Linux)

The choice of an operating system (OS) between Linux and Windows largely depends on the needs and preferences of the user. Here are some tips to help you make an informed decision.

Linux:

1. **Free and Open Source:**

2. • Linux is open-source, which means it's free, and you can customize it to meet your needs. This makes it ideal for users who want an economical system and complete control over their environment.

3. **Security and Stability:**

4. • Linux is known for its security and stability. It is less vulnerable to viruses and malware compared to Windows, making it a solid choice for servers and critical systems.

5. **Variety of Distributions:**

6. • There are many Linux distributions (such as Ubuntu, Fedora, CentOS, etc.), each with its own features. You can choose the one that best suits your needs.

7. **Development and Programming:**

8. • Linux is very popular among developers and programmers due to its wide range of available tools and compilers.

9. **Customization:**

10.• You can customize your user environment, from the graphical interface to the system kernel. This is ideal for advanced users.

11.**Hardware Compatibility:**

12.• While Linux has improved in terms of hardware compatibility, it may still face challenges when running certain applications and hardware drivers designed specifically for Windows.

Implementation Decisions

Tips for Choosing an Operating System Based on User Needs (Windows).

Windows:

Ease of Use:
• Windows is known for its intuitive user interface and is widely used in consumer and business environments. It is a solid choice if you prefer a system that simply works without the need for complex configurations.

Software Compatibility:
• Windows is compatible with a wide variety of software and games. If you have specific applications that only work on Windows, this operating system is the obvious choice.

Technical Support and Hardware Compatibility:
• Windows is often compatible with a wide range of hardware and receives extensive technical support. This is important if you need a system that works smoothly with diverse hardware.

Automatic Updates:
• Windows provides automatic updates, which can be beneficial for ensuring security and performance.

Enterprise Environment:
• Windows is widely used in corporate and business environments, making it a solid choice if you need interoperability with enterprise systems and productivity tools. Ultimately, the choice between Linux and Windows will depend on your specific needs. You can even consider using both systems in a dual-boot environment if it's relevant to your situation. It's also important to remember that in some cases, you might opt for a virtual machine or container to run the non-primary operating system on your system.

Specific Use Cases for Linux and Windows

Linux and Windows are two operating systems with different focuses and features, so there are situations where one may be preferable over the other depending on specific needs and requirements. Here are some specific use cases that highlight the advantages of one over the other

1. Software Development and Web Servers:

    - Linux: Linux is the preferred choice for software development and web server implementation due to its stability, security, and performance. Most web servers like Apache, Nginx, and MySQL run on Linux systems. Furthermore, open-source development tools are widely compatible with Linux.

2. Supercomputing and High-Performance Computing:

    - Linux: Most supercomputers and high-performance clusters run Linux distributions. Linux can be customized and fine-tuned to make the most of the hardware, making it ideal for applications that require extreme performance.

3. Gaming and Office Productivity Software:

    - Windows: Windows is the preferred platform for gaming and office productivity software. Most games are developed for Windows, and many office applications, such as Microsoft Office, are specifically designed to run on this operating system.

4. Graphic Design and Video Editing:

    - Windows and macOS: In the field of graphic design and video editing, Windows and macOS are often preferred due to the availability of professional graphic design and video editing software, such as Adobe Creative Suite and Final Cut Pro, which are not available on Linux.

5. Automation and Embedded Systems:

    - Linux: Linux is widely used in embedded systems and industrial automation due to its customization capability, stability, and ability to run on diverse hardware.

Specific Use Cases between

Part 2

6. Open Source Programming and Development:

   • Linux: Linux is the preferred choice of many developers and programmers due to its open source nature.

   • It offers a variety of open-source development tools, libraries, and integrated development environments (IDEs).

7. Security and Privacy:

   • Linux: Linux is generally considered more secure and privacy-friendly compared to Windows.

   • Linux distributions provide greater control over security and privacy settings.

8. Cost and Licensing:

   • Linux: Linux is open source and generally free, making it an attractive option in environments where licensing costs need to be minimized.

   • It's important to remember that the choice between Linux and Windows will depend on the specific requirements of each situation, as well as user preferences and experience.

   • Additionally, in many cases, it is possible to use both systems in parallel through virtualization or dual-boot configurations to take advantage of the benefits of each based on the current needs.

Cost Comparison
Part 1

nalysis of costs associated with the implementation and maintenance of each system. The cost
mparison between Linux and Windows in terms of implementation and maintenance can vary
pending on several factors, such as the intended use, company size, specific needs, and user
eferences. Here are some key aspects to consider.

Licensing

Linux:
Most Linux distributions are open source and free. There are no direct licensing costs associated
th most distributions. However, you may need to pay for technical support if you require it.

Windows:
Microsoft Windows has licensing costs. This can vary depending on the edition you choose (e.g.,
indows 10 Home, Windows 10 Pro, Windows Server, etc.) and the number of devices or users
at need licenses.

Hardware:
In terms of hardware requirements, Linux is generally lighter and can run on older or less
werful hardware compared to the latest versions of Windows. This can reduce hardware upgrade
sts.

Technical Support

Linux:
While most distributions are open source and free, you may want to hire technical support,
pecially if you are running Linux in a critical business environment. The cost of this support will
ry by provider.

Windows:
Microsoft offers paid technical support options, which can be expensive, but they also provide a
ide range of online support resources. The cost will depend on the level of support required.

Cost Comparison

Part 2

Analysis of costs associated with the implementation and maintenance of each system.

4. **Software and Applications:** In terms of software, many business applications are available for both Linux and Windows. However, some specific applications may be more readily available or compatible with Windows, which could influence costs.

5. **Updates and Maintenance:** Software and security updates are important for both platforms. Linux tends to have more frequent security updates, which may require more time and resources for maintenance.

6. **Administration and Training:** Staff training and system administration can be significant cost factors. System administrators may require specific skills and certifications to work with one platform or the other.

7. Scalability and Future Requirements: You should consider your long-term needs and how each system will adapt as your company grows. Some companies find that Linux is more scalable and adaptable to their changing needs.

8. **Virtualization and Cloud:** Both Linux and Windows are used in virtualization and cloud environments. Costs can vary depending on the platform you choose and the specific virtualization and cloud solutions you implement.

In summary, the cost comparison between Linux and Windows largely depends on your organization's needs and available resources. Linux tends to be more cost-effective in terms of licensing, but costs may increase if you require extensive technical support. Windows has more apparent licensing costs but may offer greater compatibility with certain business applications. The choice between the two operating systems should be based on a detailed analysis of your specific needs and resources.

Future Perspective

Part 1

A look at what the future could hold for Linux and Windows. The future of the Linux and Windows operating systems is an interesting and ever-evolving topic. Below, I will provide some important insights into what the future could hold for both operating systems.

Linux:

1. Growth in usage:

Linux has experienced steady growth in recent years, especially in the enterprise and server domains. This trend is likely to continue as many businesses appreciate the stability and security it offers.

2. Desktop convergence:

With projects like Ubuntu's Unity and Linux application compatibility on Chrome OS, we may see greater convergence between desktop systems and Linux-based mobile devices, leading to a more seamless user experience.

3. More gaming on Linux:

Game compatibility on Linux has significantly improved in recent years, thanks to projects like Steam's Proton. As game developers continue to adapt their titles for Linux, we may see more gamers transitioning to this platform.

4. Adoption in embedded devices and IoT:

Linux is widely used in embedded devices and the Internet of Things (IoT) due to its versatility and scalability. In the future, we are likely to see an increase in the adoption of Linux in this field as IoT technology continues to grow.

Future Outlook Part 2

Windows

1. Windows 10/11:

Microsoft continues to develop Windows 10 and Windows 11 as its primary operating systems. The company has focused on improving security, user experience, and application compatibility in these versions.

2. Cloud Services:

Microsoft is driving its cloud services through Azure, and Windows integrates closely with these services. This integration is expected to continue to grow, allowing for greater flexibility and online collaboration.

3. Windows on ARM:

Microsoft is working on making Windows more compatible with ARM processors, which could lead to a wider variety of Windows devices, such as laptops and tablets with improved battery life.

4. Augmented and Virtual Reality:

Microsoft has been developing HoloLens and Windows Mixed Reality, indicating that augmented and virtual reality will continue to be significant areas for the company in the future. In summary, the future of Linux and Windows looks promising. Linux continues to gain ground in various fields, while Microsoft continues to evolve Windows and explore new technologies. The choice between both operating systems will continue to depend on users' specific needs and the applications they use.

Conclusion Summary of Key Points and the Importance of Choosing Between Linux and Windows.

Part 1

In conclusion, the choice between Linux and Windows largely depends on individual needs and preferences. Here, we summarize the key points and the significance of this choice.

1. User Type:

    - Linux is an excellent option for advanced users and developers, while Windows is more user-friendly for the average user seeking a more familiar experience.

2. Cost:

    - Linux is open-source and generally free, making it economically attractive. Windows, on the other hand, often involves licensing costs.

3. Security:

    - Linux is known to be more secure as it is less susceptible to viruses and malware compared to Windows. However, security also depends greatly on how the system is configured and used.

4. Compatibility:

    - Windows enjoys broad compatibility with a wide range of software and hardware due to its popularity. Linux may require more effort to find specific software and compatible drivers.

5. Customization and Flexibility:

    - Linux is highly customizable and offers a variety of distributions designed for different purposes. Windows offers less flexibility in terms of customization.

6. Performance:

    - Linux tends to be more resource-efficient, making it ideal for servers and embedded systems. Windows can be more resource-intensive, which is relevant for users with limited hardware.

Conclusion Summary of Key Points and the Importance of Choosing Between

Linux and Windows.

Part 1

7. Technical Support: Windows generally has more accessible technical support and a large user base, making problem resolution easier. In Linux, support can vary depending on the distribution and the community backing it.

8. Development and Programming: Linux is a popular choice among developers due to its available development tools and environments. Windows also has development tools, but Linux is often preferred in server development environments. Ultimately, the choice between Linux and Windows will depend on your specific needs. If you're looking for a versatile, free, and highly customizable operating system, Linux may be the best choice. On the other hand, if you want a more user-friendly experience and broad compatibility with software and hardware, Windows might be the right choice. It's important to consider your goals and preferences before making a decision. NOTE: I personally, friends and acquaintances, am familiar with both operating systems, have both operating systems, and use them for different purposes, but I am a LOYAL FAN OF LINUX. I have used LINUX my entire life, and I believe that it serves the required and appropriate functions for me. However, my recommendation is that everyone should use what they need based on their finances and their work because each system has its own merits. Thank you. RX

Bibliography A list of references and resources for those interested in delving deeper into the differences between Linux and Windows

Part 1

Here I will provide you with a list of references and resources that you can consult to further investigate the differences between Linux and Windows:

1. Official Linux Website:

You can find information about different Linux distributions, documentation, and resources on the official Linux website: https://www.linux.org/

2. Official Microsoft Windows Website:

For information about Windows operating systems, official resources, and documentation, visit the Microsoft website: https://www.microsoft.com/

3. Popular Linux Distributions:

Research more about specific Linux distributions like Ubuntu, Fedora, CentOS, and more. Each of them has its own official website with detailed documentation.

4. Books on Linux and Windows:

- "Linux Bible" by Christopher Negus: A comprehensive resource for learning about Linux and its applications.
- "Windows Internals" by Mark Russinovich and David A. Solomon: Delve deep into the inner workings of Windows systems.

5. Online Communities and Forums:

- Stack Exchange - Unix & Linux: A place to ask questions and find answers related to Linux.
- Microsoft Community: A resource for getting help with Windows issues and exploring discussions about the operating system.

Bibliography List of references and resources for those interested in further research.

Part 2

6. Comparison and Analysis Sites:

DistroWatch: A website that tracks and compares different Linux distributions. TechRadar - Windows vs. Linux: An article that compares Windows and Linux on various aspects.

7. Reference Documentation:

Online Linux Documentation: The Linux Documentation Project offers a wide range of document and guides. Microsoft Technical Documentation: Find official Microsoft documentation on Windows.

8. Online Courses and Tutorials:

Platforms like Udemy, Coursera, and edX offer courses related to Linux and Windows that can delve into specific aspects of these operating systems.

9. Technical Magazines:

Magazines like "Linux Journal" and "Windows IT Pro" often have technical articles and comparisons between operating systems.

10. Blogs and YouTube Channels:

There are numerous blogs and YouTube channels dedicated to technology, where experts share the opinions and analysis of Linux and Windows. These resources will provide you with a wide range of information to thoroughly research the differences between Linux and Windows, as well as the respective features and functionalities.

Apéndices

Posibles apéndices con información técnica adicional. Aquí les dejo amigos y amigas 20 preguntas básicas sobre las diferencias y características de los sistemas operativos Linux y Windows:

Esto es para que te evalúes, a ti mismo y sepas que as aprendido y a que lógica as podido llegar con este libro, por que una ves que ayas leído este libro ya sabrás
1. ¿Cuál es la base de código subyacente de Linux y Windows?
2. ¿Quiénes son los principales desarrolladores de Linux y Windows?
3. ¿Cuál es el modelo de licencia de Linux y Windows?
4. ¿Qué es el núcleo del sistema operativo en Linux y Windows?
5. ¿Cuál es el entorno de escritorio predeterminado en Linux y Windows?
6. ¿Cuál es la principal diferencia en la gestión de archivos en Linux y Windows?
7. ¿Cómo se manejan los controladores de dispositivos en Linux y Windows?
8. ¿Cuáles son las principales diferencias en la administración de usuarios y permisos en ambos sistemas?
9. ¿Cómo se realizan las actualizaciones y parches en Linux y Windows?
10.¿Qué sistemas de archivos son más comunes en Linux y Windows?
11.¿Cuáles son las opciones de línea de comandos en Linux y Windows y cuáles son las diferencias clave?
12.¿Cómo se instalan y desinstalan aplicaciones en Linux y Windows?
13.¿Cuáles son las diferencias en cuanto a la seguridad entre Linux y Windows?
14.¿Cómo se maneja el registro del sistema en Linux y Windows?
15.¿Cuáles son las opciones de visualización en Linux y Windows?
16.¿Cómo se inicia y se apaga un sistema en Linux y Windows?
17.¿Cuáles son las diferencias en cuanto a la disponibilidad de software de terceros en Linux y Windows?
18.¿Cuál es la filosofía de actualización en Linux y Windows?
19.¿Cómo se abordan las actualizaciones de hardware en ambos sistemas?
20.¿Cuál es el enfoque de soporte técnico y comunidad en Linux y Windows?
Estas preguntas te ayudarán a explorar las diferencias y características clave entre los sistemas operativos Linux y Windows.
NOTA:
"Si has llegado a este punto de lectura en mi libro, has adquirido un valioso conocimiento sobre las diferencias entre los sistemas operativos Linux y Windows. Para asegurarte de que estás 100% convencido de cuál de estos sistemas operativos se adapta mejor a tus necesidades, te propongo una evaluación. Considera las 20 preguntas que he proporcionado para ti, reflexiona sobre tus preferencias y requisitos, y estarás en una posición sólida para tomar una decisión informada sobre si elegir Linux o Windows como tu sistema operativo preferido."

Biography

RX of Gaming RX is a passionate digital creator, a digital marketing expert, and a visionary in the world of technology. His ability to design stunning web pages, edit high-quality videos, and create exceptional digital content has made him a prominent figure in the industry. Additionally, RX is known for his expertise in operating systems and computer security.

RX of Gaming RX is the founder of three successful affiliate websites: gaminpc-rx.com, rx-fashions.com, and rxdigitaltechnology.com, which provide visitors with valuable information and high-quality products related to the gaming, fashion, and digital technology worlds. With a passion for building gaming computers, RX has proven himself to be an expert in optimizing operating systems and ensuring computer security in every project he undertakes. This book, "Two Giants Compete for Supremacy: Linux vs. Windows," is a testament to his deep knowledge and experience in the field of operating systems. Whether you are a technology enthusiast, a passionate gamer, or a digital marketing professional, this book will take you on a fascinating journey through the showdown of two computer giants, with RX of Gaming RX as your expert guide.

Printed in Great Britain
by Amazon

43877727R00030